AI Powered Leadership

Vic Beaumont

Contents

Preface.. 1

Chapter 1: The AI-assisted organisation.. 4

    Change is inevitable 4

    Technological milestones and their impact on employment................................. 4

    Roles lost to change: a historical perspective 5

    Factors contributing to role displacement today 5

    The future of work.. 6

    Data analysis and insights.. 7

    Predictive modelling 7

    Intelligent automation.. 8

    Personalised customer experiences 9

    AI assisted decision making 9

Chapter 2: Leadership in the age of AI... 16

Chapter 3: Addressing employee fears and concerns about AI.................................... 19

    Why employees fear change... 19

    What leaders can do 21

Chapter 4: The impact of AI on employee engagement and motivation...................... 26

    Managing the impact of AI on engagement and motivation................................ 29

Chapter 5: Redesigning reward and performance management................................... 33

    Challenges for traditional reward and performance management............. 33

    Redesigning reward and performance management 35

Chapter 6: Appreciative Inquiry Process 40

Preparing for AI in team development 42

Chapter 7: Using AI to improve the health of your business 45

Enhancing recruitment and talent management 45

Personalised learning and development 45

Predictive analytics for employee engagement 45

Embracing AI in the workplace 47

The 25 questions to consider before implementing AI 47

Chapter 8: The importance of a Chief AI Officer and an AI adoption plan ... 50

The role of the Chief AI Officer 50

Developing an AI adoption plan 52

Ensuring the ethical use of AI 56

Chapter 9: The future of AI and its impact on business 59

Chapter 10: Embracing the future of work 63

Preface

As we continue to observe rapid technological advancements, integrating Artificial Intelligence (AI) and automation into business operations is no longer a distant possibility but a present reality. As leaders, we stand at the threshold of a transformative period that promises to redefine how we work, compete, and innovate. Yet, with this transformation comes a host of challenges, particularly in managing the human element of our organisations. This book aims to guide leaders in considering and adopting technical solutions to advance the organisation while grappling with the impact on people in the business.

With over 30 years of experience in senior HR roles, my commitment to helping businesses become high-performing, profitable, and ethically sound is unwavering. I firmly believe embracing AI and automation is the key to achieving these goals. These emerging technologies are a strategic choice necessary for survival and growth. Failing to adapt to these new ways of working can have severe limitations, leaving businesses struggling to keep pace with their more forward-thinking competitors. This book is a call to action, urging leaders to embrace these technologies and improve their organisations.

AI and automation offer unprecedented opportunities for efficiency, innovation, and scalability. They have the potential to revolutionise the way we operate, freeing employees from mundane, repetitive tasks and allowing them to focus on more strategic, value-adding activities. This book is a testament to the transformative power of these technologies, inspiring leaders to reimagine their organisations and their employees' roles. However, the successful implementation of these technologies hinges on more than technical know-how; it requires careful consideration of the human dynamics at play. How do we prepare our employees for this change? How do we address fears of job displacement while creating a culture of continuous learning and adaptation? These questions keep me up at night and are the driving force behind this book.

Drawing on my years of experience in human resources and organisational development, I have sought to create a comprehensive roadmap for leaders. This book delves into the compelling reasons behind the necessity of adopting AI and automation, highlighting the competitive advantages and the potential for creating more meaningful and strategic roles for employees. More importantly, it offers a simple approach to managing the transition, emphasising empathy, communication, and strategic planning.

I hope you will find a wealth of insights, from identifying the right technological tools to creating a culture of innovation and resilience. I have made it my mission to provide practical strategies for reskilling your teams, maintaining morale, and ensuring a seamless transition. My goal has been to provide thoughtful advice on balancing technological advancement and human-centric leadership to build a more engaged, productive, and fulfilled workforce.

This book will give you a deeper understanding of the technological opportunities and develop the skills to lead your organisation through these changes. You will learn how to turn potential disruptions into opportunities for growth, build an adaptable and engaged team, and lead with vision and compassion in an increasingly automated world. Above all, you will discover how to create a business that succeeds financially and positively impacts the lives of its employees and the wider community.

Embrace the change but do so with a clear understanding of its implications and a steadfast commitment to your people. In doing so, you will not only navigate the complexities of AI and automation but also pave the way for a future where technology and humanity coexist harmoniously, driving your organisation towards greater success while remaining true to its core values of integrity, compassion, and excellence.

Remember, the path ahead is not always easy, but it is one that we must walk if we are to build businesses that thrive in the face of change and uncertainty. As a fellow leader and passionate advocate for employee well-being, I will support you every step of the way. Together, we can create a future where businesses adapt to the age of AI and take charge of building a better, more equitable world for all.

Chapter 1: The AI-assisted organisation

Change is inevitable

Over the past century, the world of work has undergone a remarkable transformation, driven by technological advancements that have automated tasks, streamlined processes, and rendered specific job roles obsolete. However, these changes have also paved the way for new roles in emerging fields, offering fresh opportunities for businesses and workers. From the early days of industrial automation to the rise of Artificial Intelligence and the gig economy, these changes have brought about opportunities and challenges for businesses and employees alike. This section will delve into the critical technological milestones, roles lost to change, and factors contributing to role displacement today, providing a comprehensive overview of employment.

Technological milestones and their impact on employment

The last six decades have been marked by significant technological milestones reshaping the workplace. The 1970s introduced industrial robotics, a development that revolutionised manufacturing. The 1980s brought Automated Teller Machines (ATMs) and Computer-Aided Design (CAD) software, changing how we handle money and design products. The 1990s saw the rise of Enterprise Resource Planning (ERP) systems and automated call centres, transforming business operations. The early 2000s witnessed the advent of e-commerce platforms and automated warehousing, altering the retail and logistics sectors. The 2010s saw the proliferation of AI, machine learning, self-checkout systems, autonomous vehicles, and Robotic Process Automation (RPA) tools, ushering in the era of intelligent automation. The 2020s have seen further integration of the Internet of Things (IoT) eg smart devices, AI, and robotics in manufacturing, the acceleration of remote work technologies due to the COVID-19 pandemic, and AI making inroads into creative industries and healthcare.

Roles lost to change: a historical perspective

As technology progressed, numerous job roles once integral to society became obsolete or significantly diminished. This historical perspective, from the disappearance of human alarm clocks (knocker-uppers) and lamplighters in the 1930s and 1940s to the decline of switchboard operators, typists, elevator operators, and keypunch operators in the 1970s and 80s, provides a context for the historic employment backdrop. The 1990s and 2000s saw the decline of travel agents, encyclopedia salespersons, video store clerks, bank tellers, photo lab technicians, and assembly line workers. More recently, the 2010s and 2020s have witnessed challenges for newspaper delivery jobs, travel ticket agents, parking attendants, cashiers, receptionists, and telemarketers to name a few.

Factors contributing to role displacement today

A complex interplay of factors influences role displacement in the UK. Economic pressures such as recessions, slowdowns, Brexit, inflation, and rising living costs can reduce consumer spending and force companies to cut costs, resulting in redundancies. Technological advancements in automation, AI, machine learning, and digital transformation have made specific job roles obsolete, especially those involving repetitive or routine tasks.

Globalisation has also significantly contributed to role displacement. Outsourcing and offshoring to countries with lower labour costs have led to redundancies in the UK workforce. Global supply chain disruptions have also impacted businesses and led to job cuts. Structural changes in the economy, such as the decline of traditional industries and the rise of the gig economy, have altered employment patterns, often at the cost of full-time, stable jobs.

Policy and regulatory factors, including government austerity measures, budget cuts, and regulatory standards or environmental compliance changes, can impact business operations and lead to redundancies. Market dynamics, such as industry consolidation, mergers, and shifts in consumer behaviour, have contributed to job losses in sectors like brick-and-mortar retail.

The COVID-19 pandemic has profoundly impacted employment, leading to widespread redundancies due to lockdowns, reduced demand, and changes in consumer behaviour. Lastly, the rapid pace of technological change has created a skills mismatch, where the workforce lacks the necessary skills for emerging job roles, leading to unemployment and underemployment.

By understanding these factors, business leaders can make informed decisions about implementing AI and automation in their organisations. This knowledge will help them navigate the challenges and opportunities the evolving employment landscape presents.

The future of work

As Artificial Intelligence (AI) continues to advance and integrate into the DNA of modern business, organisations increasingly recognise the potential for AI to revolutionise how work is done. In the AI-assisted organisation of the future, AI will not only automate routine tasks but also augment human capabilities, enabling employees to focus on higher-value, strategic work.

Data analysis and insights

Data analysis and insights are vital areas where AI will play a significant role. With the exponential growth of data generated by businesses, AI algorithms can process and analyse vast amounts of structured and unstructured data, uncovering patterns, trends, and correlations that may be difficult for humans to detect. This will enable organisations to make data-driven decisions, optimise processes, and identify new opportunities for growth and innovation.

Google, for example, has leveraged AI capabilities in its search algorithms, Google Photos (image recognition), and DeepMind (AlphaGo) to improve user experiences and efficiency and drive innovation. While AI has automated many routine tasks, it has also created new roles in AI development, data science, and machine learning, involving more strategic and creative responsibilities for employees.

Predictive modelling

AI-powered predictive modelling will help organisations anticipate future trends, customer behaviour, and market dynamics. By analysing historical data and identifying patterns, AI algorithms can generate accurate predictions and forecasts, enabling businesses to adapt to changing circumstances and mitigate potential risks proactively. This will be particularly valuable in demand forecasting, resource planning, and risk management.

Amazon, for example, uses AI for product recommendations, Alexa voice assistant, and logistics and supply chain management. AI has enhanced customer experiences through personalised recommendations and streamlined operations, such as faster delivery times and efficient inventory management. In its warehouses, AI-powered robots assist with picking and packing, improving productivity. While automation and AI have led to the creation of new technical roles, there are ongoing concerns about the displacement of lower-skilled jobs. To address this, Amazon has invested in retraining programs to help employees transition to new roles.

Intelligent automation

AI will drive the next wave of intelligent automation, going beyond simple rule-based automation to more complex and adaptive forms of automation. AI-powered systems can learn from data, improve over time, and handle various tasks and exceptions. This will enable organisations to streamline processes, reduce errors, and improve efficiency across multiple functions, from customer service and finance to supply chain management and HR.

IBM's Watson AI, for instance, is used for various applications, including healthcare diagnostics, financial services, and customer service chatbots. Watson has improved decision-making and efficiency in sectors like healthcare by aiding in diagnostics and treatment recommendations. It has also enhanced customer service through AI-driven chatbots that handle routine inquiries. For IBM employees, AI has enabled them to focus on more complex problem-solving tasks while automating repetitive processes, driving the need for employees skilled in AI and data analytics.

Personalised customer experiences

AI will play a crucial role in delivering personalised and engaging customer experiences. By analysing customer data, preferences, and behaviour, AI algorithms can generate personalised recommendations, tailor content and offers, and provide proactive customer support. This will help organisations build stronger customer relationships, increase loyalty, and drive revenue growth.

Microsoft, for example, integrates AI across its products like Office 365 (e.g., AI-powered features in Word and Excel), Azure AI services, and CoPilot. These AI-driven tools have improved productivity by offering advanced features like real-time grammar checks, predictive text, and data visualisations. Azure AI services enable businesses to build and deploy their own AI models. As a result, Microsoft employees are increasingly working on AI-related projects, creating opportunities in AI research, development, and deployment.

AI assisted decision making

AI will increasingly assist and augment human decision-making processes. By providing real-time insights, recommendations, and scenario modelling, AI can help leaders make more informed and data-driven decisions. This will be particularly valuable in complex and fast-paced businesses, where quick and accurate decision-making is critical to success.

Tesla uses AI for autonomous driving through its Full Self-Driving (FSD) software and for manufacturing automation. AI has been crucial in developing Tesla's autonomous driving capabilities and enhancing vehicle safety and driving experience. In manufacturing, AI-driven robots have increased production efficiency and quality. While AI has led to the creation of specialised roles in AI and robotics engineering, the automation of manufacturing processes has also raised concerns about job displacement for assembly line workers.

The future of human-run call centres is another area where AI is expected to have a significant impact. While it's unlikely that human-run call centres will become completely extinct in the next ten years, the increasing use of AI and automation technologies will drive significant changes in their structure and functioning. AI-powered chatbots and virtual assistants are already handling routine inquiries and providing 24/7 support, reducing the workload for human agents. As Natural Language Processing (NLP) advances, AI systems can handle more complex interactions and provide a more human-like experience, reducing the need for human agents.

However, human agents' roles will evolve, focusing on more complex and nuanced issues that require empathy, critical thinking, and problem-solving skills. Many call centres may adopt a hybrid model where AI handles initial customer interactions and escalates more complex issues to human agents, optimising efficiency while still providing high-quality customer service. To adapt to these changes, human agents must develop new skills, such as managing AI systems, data analysis, and emotional intelligence.

The impact of AI and automation on software developers, coders, and similar roles is also complex. While some may fear job displacement, the reality is more nuanced. AI-powered development tools, like GitHub Copilot, assist developers by auto-completing code snippets, suggesting code improvements, and generating entire functions based on comments or descriptions. These tools help speed up the coding process, reduce errors, and allow developers to focus on more complex and creative aspects of development.

With businesses' increased adoption of AI, the demand for professionals with expertise in AI, machine learning, and data science is rising. This shift creates new job opportunities and leads developers to transition from routine coding to more strategic roles. These roles include designing system architecture, ensuring system integration, and optimising performance, highlighting the evolving nature of the industry and the need for continuous learning.

However, developers must understand that the AI field is constantly evolving, and they must be committed to continuous learning to keep pace with these changes. Combining coding skills with data analytics, cybersecurity, and cloud computing knowledge will become increasingly important. While AI can automate routine and repetitive coding tasks, potentially reducing the need for entry-level developers who primarily handle such tasks, the overall demand for skilled developers is expected to grow, particularly in areas involving AI, machine learning, and data science.

Real-world examples across various industries vividly demonstrate the transformative impact of AI adoption. In healthcare, for instance, IBM Watson Health uses AI for medical imaging analysis, drug discovery, and personalised treatment plans. This accelerates diagnosis and treatment processes, improves patient outcomes, and reduces operational costs. Automating some diagnostic tasks allows healthcare professionals to focus more on patient care, complex case management, and leveraging AI insights to make informed decisions. This underscores the role of AI in enhancing human capabilities and the value it brings to the healthcare industry.

In retail, Walmart uses AI for inventory management, customer service chatbots, and personalised shopping experiences. AI-driven inventory management systems optimise stock levels, reducing waste and ensuring product availability. Chatbots enhance customer service by handling routine inquiries, and AI-powered recommendation engines drive sales by suggesting relevant products. Store associates are shifting from routine tasks to roles that require customer interaction and problem-solving, and there is an increased need for data analysts and AI system managers.

The manufacturing sector is also witnessing significant changes driven by AI. Siemens, for example, uses AI for predictive maintenance, quality control, and supply chain optimisation. Predictive maintenance reduces downtime by predicting equipment failures before they happen, while AI-driven quality control systems detect defects in real-time, ensuring high product quality. Supply chain optimisation minimises costs and improves efficiency. As a result, workers are transitioning from manual tasks to roles that involve overseeing and maintaining AI systems, with an increased focus on continuous improvement and innovation.

The AI-assisted organisation of the future will be characterised by a seamless integration of human and machine intelligence, where AI augments and empowers employees to achieve new levels of productivity, innovation, and value creation. AI adoption drives significant changes in business operations and employees. While some routine tasks are automated, new opportunities are emerging for employees to focus on higher-level functions requiring creativity, problem-solving, and human interaction.

Organisations must adopt a proactive and strategic approach to AI adoption. This involves assessing current processes, identifying areas where AI can deliver the most value, developing a clear AI strategy and roadmap, and investing in the necessary infrastructure and talent to support AI initiatives. By building an AI-ready culture where employees are encouraged to embrace change, continuously learn and upskill, and collaborate with AI systems, organisations can prepare for this transformative shift and ensure the success of their AI initiatives.

By proactively preparing for the AI-assisted future and embracing AI's potential, organisations can position themselves for success. As AI advances and reshapes industries, the key to thriving in this new era will be a commitment to continuous learning, adaptability, and a willingness to reinvent how we work. This emphasis on constant learning and adaptability underscores the urgency of staying updated in the rapid and continuous AI era, motivating us to invest in our professional development and stay ahead of the curve.

The rapid advancement of Artificial Intelligence (AI) is transforming business, offering organisations unprecedented opportunities for growth, efficiency, and innovation. As AI technologies become more sophisticated and accessible, companies across industries recognise AI's potential to revolutionise how work is done and value is created.

However, integrating AI into business operations also presents significant challenges and considerations, particularly regarding its impact on employees. While AI has the potential to automate specific tasks and augment human capabilities, it is crucial to recognise that the role of human employees remains vital in an AI-driven organisation.

The shift towards AI-assisted organisations requires a thoughtful and strategic approach that balances AI's benefits with employees' needs and concerns. Leaders must navigate the complexities of AI adoption while ensuring that their employees are supported, engaged, and motivated throughout the transition. This reassures employees that their well-being and professional growth are integral to the organisation's AI strategy, fostering a sense of value and security.

Scenario 1: StellarSoft Solutions

StellarSoft Solutions, a global financial services company, recognised the potential for AI to transform its operations and drive competitive advantage. However, the company also understood the importance of balancing AI adoption with the needs and concerns of its employees.

StellarSoft Solutions developed a comprehensive AI adoption strategy, prioritising employee engagement and support to navigate this challenge. The company invested in extensive communication and training programs to help employees understand the benefits of AI and how it would augment, rather than replace, their roles.

It also established an AI Centre of Excellence (CoE) to provide ongoing support and resources for employees as they adapted to working with AI technologies. The CoE offered training and skill development opportunities and forums for employees to share their experiences and concerns.

The company maintained a strong focus on employee engagement and motivation throughout the AI adoption process. The company implemented various initiatives to recognise and reward employees for their contributions, including AI-assisted performance management and personalised career development paths.

Because of its employee-centric approach to AI adoption, StellarSoft Solutions successfully navigated the transition to an AI-assisted organisation. The company achieved significant improvements in efficiency and productivity while maintaining high levels of employee engagement and job satisfaction. StellarSoft Solutions's success story demonstrates the importance of prioritising employee needs and concerns in an AI-driven organisation.

By recognising the challenges and opportunities presented by AI and adopting an employee-centric approach to AI adoption, organisations can harness AI's transformative potential while ensuring their employees' continued engagement and motivation.

Chapter 2: Leadership in the age of AI

Adopting Artificial Intelligence (AI) is not merely a technological advancement; it represents a fundamental shift in how organisations operate, make decisions, and create value. As AI increasingly integrates into business, leaders must adapt their strategies, skills, and mindsets to navigate this transformation effectively. The transition to becoming an AI-assisted organisation is a significant undertaking that will profoundly impact leadership and management practices across various dimensions.

One key area where AI will substantially impact decision-making processes is data analysis. Leaders will increasingly rely on AI-driven analytics to make data-driven decisions, leading to more accurate and timely insights. This shift requires managers to become proficient in interpreting data and understanding AI-generated insights, emphasising the importance of data literacy training. AI's ability to process vast amounts of information quickly will enable faster decision-making and more agile responses to market changes, challenging leaders to adapt to a more rapid pace and make strategic decisions more dynamically.

Talent management is another critical area that will undergo significant changes in the AI-assisted organisation. As AI automates many routine tasks, employees must shift towards more complex and creative roles. Leaders must prioritise reskilling and upskilling initiatives to prepare employees for these new responsibilities, promoting a culture of continuous learning and development. Additionally, the growing demand for AI and data science expertise will require leaders to develop strategies for competitive talent acquisition, including partnerships with educational institutions and investment in internal training programs.

The transition to an AI-assisted organisation also necessitates a shift in organisational culture. AI has the potential to drive innovation by enabling new business models, products, and services, but this requires a culture that encourages experimentation and continuous improvement. Leaders must create an environment where experimentation is valued and failures are seen as learning opportunities, which requires openness to change and challenge the status quo. Furthermore, leaders must ensure that employees understand how AI will enhance rather than replace their roles, maintaining transparent communication and involvement in the AI integration process to foster employee engagement.

Ethical considerations and responsible AI use become paramount. Leaders must establish ethical guidelines and governance structures to address bias, privacy, and transparency. This may involve creating roles such as AI ethics officers and ensuring compliance with regulatory standards. Building trust in AI systems is crucial for employee and customer acceptance, requiring leaders to be transparent about how AI is used and to make efforts to demystify AI technologies.

Effective leadership demands a clear strategic vision and the ability to align AI initiatives with overall business objectives. This requires a forward-thinking mindset and the capacity to communicate a compelling vision that motivates and inspires the entire organisation. Successful AI implementation often relies on cross-functional collaboration, necessitating leaders to break down silos and develop a collaborative culture.

AI presents opportunities for operational efficiency, such as process optimisation and enhanced performance metrics. Leaders must identify key areas where AI can add value and oversee the integration of AI technologies into existing workflows, continuously monitoring and optimising to realise the full benefits. Adapting performance metrics to include AI-driven insights and ensuring alignment with strategic objectives will be crucial in measuring success.

The shift to an AI-assisted organisation represents a significant transformation, reshaping leadership and management practices. From decision-making processes and talent management to organisational culture and ethical considerations, leaders must navigate many challenges and opportunities. By developing the necessary skills, a culture of innovation and continuous learning, and maintaining a strong moral compass, leaders can successfully guide their organisations through this transformative journey and harness the power of AI to drive growth, efficiency, and competitive advantage.

Chapter 3: Addressing employee fears and concerns about AI

As organisations begin to action their AI adoption plans, addressing employees' fears and concerns is one of their most significant challenges. The prospect of AI integration can trigger various emotions among employees, from uncertainty and anxiety to outright resistance and fear of job displacement.

Leaders must recognise and proactively address these fears and concerns to ensure a smooth and successful transition to an AI-assisted organisation. By understanding the root causes of employee apprehension and implementing strategies to mitigate them, leaders can build trust, promote engagement, and create a positive and supportive environment for AI adoption.

Why employees fear change

Resistance to change is a natural human response, mainly when it involves significant shifts in how work is done and the role of employees in the organisation. Some of the key reasons why employees fear change include:

1. Uncertainty and ambiguity: Employees may feel uncertain about how AI will impact their roles, responsibilities, and job security, leading to anxiety and stress.

2. Skill obsolescence: The integration of AI may require employees to acquire new skills and competencies, leading to fears of skill obsolescence and the need for significant upskilling or reskilling.

3. Loss of control and autonomy: AI-assisted decision-making and automation may be perceived as reducing employee autonomy and control over their work, leading to concerns about diminished job satisfaction and engagement.
4. Ethical concerns: Employees may have concerns about the ethical implications of AI, such as data privacy, algorithmic bias, and the potential for unintended consequences.

Scenario 2: Quantum Innovations

Quantum Innovations, a global manufacturing company, recognised the need to address employee fears and concerns as it embarked on its AI adoption journey. The company had announced plans to implement AI-powered automation and decision-making systems, leading to significant employee apprehension.

To address these concerns, Quantum Innovations implemented a comprehensive change management strategy prioritising employee communication, engagement, and support. The company conducted a series of town hall meetings and workshops to provide employees with transparent information about the AI adoption process, including the rationale for AI integration, the expected benefits, and the potential impact on roles and responsibilities.

The company also established an AI literacy program to help employees understand the basics of AI technology and how it could augment and enhance their work. The program included training modules, hands-on workshops, and access to AI experts who could answer questions and provide guidance.

Quantum Innovations implemented a robust reskilling and upskilling program to address concerns about job security and skill obsolescence. The company provided employees with opportunities to acquire new skills and competencies relevant to working with AI. It offered clear career development paths aligned with the company's AI adoption roadmap.

They maintained open and transparent communication channels throughout the AI adoption process, encouraging employees to share their concerns and feedback. The company also celebrated successes and milestones, recognising employees' contributions to the AI-driven transformation.

As a result of its proactive and employee-centric approach to change management, Quantum Innovations successfully navigated the transition to an AI-assisted organisation. The company achieved significant improvements in efficiency and productivity while maintaining high levels of employee engagement and job satisfaction. Quantum Innovations success story demonstrates the importance of addressing employee fears and concerns in AI adoption.

What leaders can do

Leaders must adopt a proactive and empathetic approach that prioritises communication, transparency, and support to address employee fears and concerns about AI effectively. Some key strategies leaders can employ include:

1. Communicate transparently

Provide clear and transparent information about the AI adoption process, including the rationale for AI integration, the expected benefits, and the potential impact on roles and responsibilities.

Practical tips for transparent communication

- Develop a comprehensive communication plan that outlines key messages, channels, and timelines for sharing information about AI adoption.
- Conduct regular town hall meetings, webinars, or Q&A sessions to provide updates on the AI adoption process and address employee questions and concerns.
- Create a dedicated AI adoption portal or resource centre where employees can access information, FAQs, and training materials related to AI integration.
- Ensure that communication is two-way by providing opportunities for employees to share their feedback, concerns, and ideas through surveys, focus groups, or suggestion boxes.

2. Engage employees in the process

Involve employees in AI adoption, seeking input and feedback on critical decisions and implementation plans. This can help build trust and ownership in the process.

Practical tips for employee engagement

- Establish an AI adoption steering committee that includes representatives from different functions and levels of the organisation to provide input and guidance on the AI adoption process.
- Conduct workshops or planning sessions where employees can contribute ideas and suggestions for leveraging AI to improve processes, products, or services.
- Encourage employees to participate in pilot projects or proof-of-concept initiatives related to AI adoption, allowing them to gain hands-on experience and provide feedback on the technology.

- Recognise and celebrate employees actively engaging in the AI adoption process, highlighting their contributions and value to the organisation.

3. Provide training and skill development

Invest in comprehensive training and skill development programs to help employees acquire the competencies to work effectively with AI technologies.

Practical tips for training and skill development

- Conduct a skills gap analysis to identify the competencies and skills required for employees to work effectively with AI technologies.
- Develop a comprehensive training curriculum that includes technical and soft skills training, such as data literacy, critical thinking, and problem-solving.
- Offer a variety of training formats, such as in-person workshops, online courses, and on-the-job learning opportunities, to cater to different learning styles and preferences.
- Provide opportunities for employees to apply their newly acquired skills through hands-on projects, hackathons, or innovation challenges.
- Encourage employees to pursue certifications or advanced degrees in AI and data science, providing financial support or time off for learning and development.

4. Offer support and resources

Provide employees with access to support and resources, such as AI experts, change management coaches, and employee assistance programs, to help them navigate the transition.

Practical tips for offering support and resources

- Establish an AI Centre of Excellence or a dedicated AI support team that employees can contact for guidance, troubleshooting, or advice related to AI technologies.
- Provide access to change management coaches or mentors who can help employees navigate the emotional and psychological aspects of the AI adoption process.
- Offer employee assistance programs or counselling services to support employees experiencing stress, anxiety, or other mental health concerns related to the AI transition.
- Create peer support networks or employee resource groups where employees can connect with others who are going through similar experiences and share best practices or coping strategies.

5. Recognise and celebrate success

Celebrate successes and milestones along the AI adoption journey, recognising employees' contributions and reinforcing the benefits of AI integration.

Practical tips for recognising and celebrating success

- Establish clear metrics and milestones for measuring the success of AI adoption initiatives, such as increased efficiency, improved customer satisfaction, or reduced costs.
- Regularly communicate progress and successes related to AI adoption through company-wide emails, newsletters, or town hall meetings.
- Recognise and reward employees who have contributed significantly to the AI adoption process, such as those who have led successful pilot projects or developed innovative AI solutions.

- Celebrate critical milestones in the AI adoption journey, such as launching a new AI-powered product or completing a significant training program through company-wide events or celebrations.
- Share success stories and case studies highlighting the positive impact of AI adoption on the organisation, employees, and customers, reinforcing the technology's value and benefits.

By proactively addressing employee fears and concerns about AI, leaders can create a positive and supportive environment for AI adoption, promoting engagement, motivation, and success in the AI-driven organisation.

Chapter 4: The impact of AI on employee engagement and motivation

Integrating AI into business operations has significant implications for employee engagement and motivation. While AI has the potential to automate specific tasks and augment human capabilities, leaders must understand and manage the impact of AI on their employees' psychological and emotional well-being.

On the positive side, AI can enhance employee engagement and motivation by:

1. Enabling more meaningful work

By automating routine and repetitive tasks, AI can free employees to focus on more strategic, creative, and value-added activities, increasing job satisfaction and engagement.

2. Providing real-time feedback and coaching

AI-powered performance management systems can provide employees with real-time feedback and coaching, helping them continuously improve their skills and performance.

3. Offering personalised learning and development

AI can enable personalised learning and development experiences tailored to each employee's unique needs and preferences, increasing motivation and engagement in skill acquisition.

4. Enhancing work-life balance

AI-assisted scheduling and workflow management can help optimise workloads and ensure a better balance between work and personal life, reducing stress and burnout.

However, AI can also have negative impacts on employee engagement and motivation, such as:

1. Job insecurity and anxiety

The fear of job displacement and skill obsolescence can lead to increased anxiety and stress among employees, negatively impacting engagement and motivation.

2. Reduced autonomy and control

AI-assisted decision-making and automation may be perceived as reducing employee autonomy and control over their work, leading to decreased job satisfaction and engagement.

3. Impersonal and transactional relationships

The increased reliance on AI systems for communication and collaboration may lead to more impersonal and transactional relationships among employees, reducing social connection and engagement.

Scenario 3: Zenith Robotics

Zenith Robotics, a global technology company, recognised the importance of actively managing AI's impact on employee engagement and motivation. As the company integrated AI technologies, it implemented various strategies to ensure employees remained engaged, motivated, and emotionally connected to their work.

One key initiative was the creation of AI-assisted "engagement champions" within each department. These champions monitored employee sentiment and engagement levels using AI-powered sentiment analysis tools and regular pulse surveys. They provided feedback and recommendations to leadership on addressing any emerging concerns or issues.

Zenith Robotics also implemented an AI-powered performance management system that provided employees real-time feedback and coaching. The system used machine learning algorithms to analyse employee performance data and provide personalised recommendations for improving and recognising achievements and milestones.

Zenith Robotics invested heavily in reskilling and upskilling programs to address concerns about job security and skill changes, offering employees a range of learning and development opportunities to acquire new competencies and stay ahead of the curve. The company also implemented an AI-powered career development platform that provided employees with personalised career guidance and job recommendations based on their skills, interests, and aspirations.

Zenith Robotics maintained a strong focus on employee well-being and work-life balance throughout the AI adoption process. The company used AI-assisted scheduling and workflow management tools to optimise workloads and ensure that employees had sufficient time for rest, relaxation, and personal pursuits.

As a result of these efforts, Zenith Robotics successfully maintained high levels of employee engagement and motivation throughout its AI adoption journey. The company's attrition rates remained low, and employee satisfaction scores consistently exceeded industry benchmarks. Zenith Robotics's success story demonstrates the importance of proactively managing AI's impact on employee engagement and motivation in an AI-driven organisation.

Managing the impact of AI on engagement and motivation

To effectively manage the impact of AI on employee engagement and motivation, leaders must adopt a holistic and human-centric approach that prioritises their employees' psychological and emotional well-being. Some key strategies leaders can employ include:

1. Communicate the benefits of AI

Help employees understand how AI can enhance their work experience and enable them to focus on more meaningful and rewarding activities.

Practical tips for communicating the benefits of AI

- Develop clear and compelling messaging highlighting how AI can augment and enhance human capabilities rather than replace them.
- Share case studies and success stories demonstrating how AI has helped employees be more productive, creative, and effective.
- Encourage employees to share their experiences and insights on how AI has positively impacted their work and career development.
- Regularly communicate updates and progress on AI initiatives, highlighting the benefits and value that AI is bringing to the organisation and its employees.

2. Provide ongoing support and resources

To help employees navigate the transition, offer them access to support and resources, such as AI literacy programs, change management coaching, and mental health services.

Practical tips for providing ongoing support and resources

- Establish an AI literacy program that helps employees understand the basics of AI technology, its applications, and its potential impact on their roles and the organisation.
- Offer change management coaching and support to help employees navigate the emotional and psychological aspects of the AI transition, such as anxiety, stress, or resistance to change.
- Provide access to mental health services and resources, such as employee assistance programs, counselling services, or mindfulness and stress management training.
- Create a network of AI champions or mentors who can guide, support, and advise employees throughout the AI adoption process.

3. Promote a culture of lifelong learning

Encourage and support continuous learning and skill development, which will help employees stay ahead of the curve and remain engaged and motivated in their work.

Practical tips for developing a culture of lifelong learning

- Develop a comprehensive learning and development strategy that prioritises continuous skill acquisition and growth and is aligned with the needs of the AI-driven organisation.
- To cater to different learning styles and preferences, offer various learning and development opportunities, such as in-person training, online courses, workshops, and conferences.
- Encourage employees to pursue certifications, advanced degrees, or other professional development opportunities related to AI and emerging technologies.

- Recognise and reward employees who actively engage in learning and skill development, highlighting the value and importance of continuous growth and adaptation.

4. Emphasise the importance of human connection

Prioritise and facilitate human connection and collaboration, even as AI technologies become more prevalent in the workplace.

Practical tips for emphasising the importance of human connection

- Encourage regular team-building activities, social events, and opportunities for employees to connect and build relationships outside work.
- Encourage employees to collaborate on projects and initiatives that leverage human and AI capabilities to promote a culture of collaboration and teamwork.
- Provide opportunities for employees to share their experiences, insights, and best practices related to working with AI technologies, developing a sense of community and shared learning.
- Recognise and celebrate human employees' unique contributions and value to the organisation, emphasising the importance of creativity, empathy, and emotional intelligence.

5. Monitor and address engagement levels

Monitor employee engagement and motivation levels regularly using AI-powered sentiment analysis tools and pulse surveys, and take proactive steps to address any emerging concerns or issues.

Practical tips for monitoring and addressing engagement levels

- Implement AI-powered sentiment analysis tools that can help to identify patterns and trends in employee feedback, comments, and interactions, providing insights into engagement and motivation levels.

- Conduct regular pulse surveys to gather employee feedback and insights on their experiences, concerns, and suggestions about AI adoption and its impact on their work and well-being.
- Establish clear metrics and KPIs for measuring employee engagement and motivation, such as employee net promoter score (NPS), attrition rates, or employee satisfaction scores.
- Create a dedicated team or task force responsible for monitoring and addressing employee engagement and motivation levels, providing regular reports and recommendations to leadership on areas for improvement or intervention.
- Take proactive steps to address any concerns or issues that emerge, such as providing additional support and resources, adjusting AI adoption strategies, or implementing new initiatives to boost engagement and motivation.

By proactively managing AI's impact on employee engagement and motivation, leaders can create a positive and supportive environment that enables their employees to thrive in the age of AI.

Chapter 5: Redesigning reward and performance management

Integrating AI into business operations has significant implications for reward and performance management practices. As AI technologies automate specific tasks and augment human capabilities, traditional approaches to evaluating and rewarding employee performance may no longer be sufficient.

Challenges for traditional reward and performance management

Some of the critical challenges that AI poses for traditional reward and performance management practices include:

1. Shifting job roles and responsibilities

As AI automates specific tasks and creates new roles and responsibilities, traditional job descriptions and performance metrics may become less relevant or accurate.

2. Increased emphasis on soft skills

With AI handling many routine and repetitive tasks, the value of soft skills such as creativity, emotional intelligence, and adaptability may increase, requiring new approaches to evaluating and rewarding these competencies.

3. Need for real-time feedback and coaching

The pace of change in an AI-driven organisation may require more frequent and real-time feedback and coaching than traditional annual performance reviews.

4. Potential for algorithmic bias

AI-powered performance management systems may introduce algorithmic bias, requiring careful monitoring and mitigation to ensure fairness and equity.

Scenario 4: NexaTech

NexaTech, a global education services company, recognised the need to redesign its reward and performance management practices as it integrated AI technologies. The company had traditionally relied on annual performance reviews and fixed bonus structures but recognised that these approaches were no longer sufficient in the age of AI.

To address this challenge, NexaTech implemented various innovative strategies to align its reward and performance management practices with the needs of an AI-driven organisation. One key initiative was adopting an AI-powered continuous performance management system that provided employees real-time feedback and coaching based on various data points, including customer feedback, project outcomes, and collaboration metrics.

NexaTech also redesigned its job competencies to emphasise the importance of soft skills and adaptability, creating new roles and career paths that value these competencies alongside technical expertise. The company implemented a skills-based pay system that rewarded employees for acquiring and applying new skills rather than solely based on KPIs and project outcomes.

To address concerns about algorithmic bias, NexaTech established a dedicated AI ethics committee responsible for monitoring and auditing the company's AI-powered performance management systems. The committee worked closely with HR and business leaders to ensure these systems were fair, transparent, and aligned with the company's values and goals.

As a result of these efforts, NexaTech successfully transformed its reward and performance management practices to support the needs of an AI-driven organisation. Employee engagement and satisfaction scores increased, and the company was able to attract and retain top talent in a highly competitive market. NexaTech's success story demonstrates the importance of reimagining reward and performance management practices in the age of AI.

Redesigning reward and performance management

To effectively align reward and performance management practices with the needs of an AI-driven organisation, leaders must adopt a proactive and innovative approach that prioritises fairness, transparency, and continuous improvement. Some key strategies leaders can employ include:

1. Adopt AI-powered continuous performance management

Implement AI-powered performance management systems that provide employees real-time feedback and coaching based on various data points and metrics.

Practical tips for adopting AI-powered continuous performance management

- Identify the key data points and metrics most relevant and predictive of employee performance in an AI-driven organisation, such as customer feedback, project outcomes, and collaboration metrics.

- Develop or acquire an AI-powered performance management platform to collect, analyse, and provide real-time insights based on these data points.
- Train managers and employees to use the platform effectively, guiding them in interpreting and acting on the insights and feedback provided.
- Establish clear guidelines and protocols for using the platform, ensuring it is used consistently and fairly across the organisation.
- Regularly review and update the platform based on feedback and insights from employees and managers, ensuring that it remains relevant and effective over time.

2. Emphasise soft skills and adaptability

Redesign job roles and career paths to emphasise the importance of soft skills and adaptability and reward employees for acquiring and applying these competencies.

Practical tips for emphasising soft skills and adaptability

- Conduct a comprehensive review of job descriptions and competency frameworks to identify the most critical soft skills and adaptability competencies for success in an AI-driven organisation.
- Develop new job architectures and career paths that prioritise these competencies, creating opportunities for employees to develop and apply these skills.
- Implement a skills-based pay system that rewards employees for acquiring and applying new skills and competencies rather than solely based on KPIs or outcomes.

- Provide training and development opportunities to develop soft skills and adaptability, such as workshops on creativity, emotional intelligence, or change management.
- Recognise and celebrate employees who demonstrate exceptional soft skills and adaptability, highlighting their contributions and the value they bring to the organisation.

3. Consider skills-based pay

Adopt skills-based pay systems that reward employees for acquiring and applying new skills rather than solely based on delivery and performance metrics.

Practical tips for implementing skills-based pay

- Conduct a comprehensive skills inventory to identify the essential skills and competencies that are most valuable and in demand in an AI-driven organisation.
- Develop a skills framework that outlines the different proficiency levels for each skill and the associated pay ranges or bonuses for each level.
- Communicate the skills framework and pay system clearly to employees and provide guidance on how to acquire and demonstrate new skills and competencies.
- Implement a system for assessing and certifying employee skills through assessments, certifications, or peer reviews.
- Regularly review and update the skills framework and pay system based on changing business needs and market trends to ensure they remain relevant and competitive.

4. Ensure fairness and transparency

Establish dedicated AI ethics committees to monitor and audit AI-powered performance management systems, ensuring fairness, transparency, and alignment with organisational values and goals.

Practical tips for ensuring fairness and transparency

- Establish clear principles and guidelines for the ethical use of AI in performance management, such as ensuring that the systems are unbiased, transparent, and accountable.
- Appoint a dedicated AI ethics committee with representatives from HR, legal, IT, and business functions and external experts or advisors.
- Conduct regular audits and assessments of AI-powered performance management systems to identify and mitigate potential biases or unintended consequences.
- Provide training and education to employees and managers on the principles of ethical AI and how to use AI-powered systems fairly and responsibly.
- Establish clear channels for employees to report any concerns or issues related to using AI in performance management and take prompt action to address any violations or misconduct.

5. Promote a continuous learning and growth culture

Encourage and reward continuous learning and skill development, which will help employees stay ahead of the curve and remain engaged and motivated.

Practical tips for developing a culture of continuous learning and growth

- Develop a comprehensive learning and development strategy that prioritises continuous skill acquisition and growth and is aligned with the needs of the AI-driven organisation.
- To cater to different learning styles and preferences, offer various learning and development opportunities, such as in-person training, online courses, workshops, and conferences.
- Encourage employees to pursue certifications, advanced degrees, or other professional development opportunities related to AI and emerging technologies.
- Recognise and reward employees who actively engage in learning and skill development, highlighting the value and importance of continuous growth and adaptation.
- Provide opportunities for employees to apply their new skills and knowledge in real-world projects or initiatives, developing a sense of purpose and impact in their work.

By redesigning reward and performance management practices to align with the needs of an AI-driven organisation, leaders can create a positive and supportive environment that enables their employees to thrive in the age of AI. This approach supports employee engagement and motivation and positions the organisation for success in a rapidly changing and competitive market.

Chapter 6: Appreciative Inquiry Process

Appreciative Inquiry is a strengths-based approach to organisational development and change management that focuses on identifying and leveraging an organisation's or team's positive aspects.

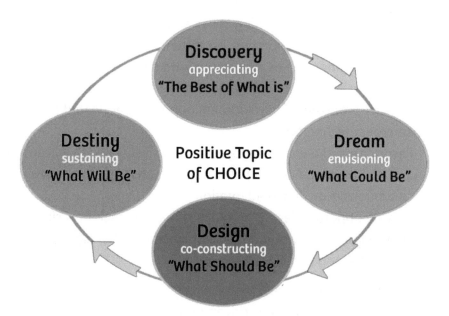

The Appreciative Inquiry process typically involves four stages, often referred to as the 4-D cycle:

1. **Discovery:** This stage involves identifying and appreciating the best of what is. Team members share stories of peak experiences and successful practices, uncovering the organisation's core strengths and values.

2. **Dream:** In this stage, participants envision the organisation's future. They imagine what the organisation could look like if it were at its best, developing creativity and collective aspiration.

3. **Design:** Here, the focus shifts to planning and prioritising. Participants co-create actionable strategies and initiatives to help achieve the envisioned future, aligning these plans with the strengths identified during the Discovery phase.
4. **Destiny/Delivery:** The final stage involves implementing the designed initiatives and sustaining the momentum. This phase is about making the envisioned future a reality through continuous learning, adaptation, and innovation.

Scenario 5: Ecofusion

Ecofusion, a healthcare services provider, faced challenges related to employee morale, patient satisfaction, and operational efficiency. The leadership team embarked on an Appreciative Inquiry (AI) process to drive positive change and tap into the organisation's strengths.

During the Discovery phase, employees shared stories of exceptional patient care, successful collaborations, and moments of pride in their work. These stories revealed Ecofusion's core strengths, including its dedicated employees, patient-centric culture, and commitment to innovation.

In the Dream phase, employees envisioned a future where Ecofusion was recognised as a leader in patient care and employee satisfaction. They imagined a workplace where collaboration, continuous learning, and employee well-being were prioritised.

Moving into the Design phase, cross-functional teams co-created strategies and initiatives to bring the envisioned future to life. These included implementing a patient feedback system, launching an employee recognition program, and investing in technology to streamline operations.

Finally, in the Destiny/Delivery phase, Ecofusion implemented the designed initiatives. Pilot projects were launched, progress was regularly reviewed, and successes were celebrated. The company is also committed to ongoing learning and adaptation to sustain the positive changes.

As a result of the appreciative inquiry process, Ecofusion experienced a significant transformation. Employee engagement increased, patient satisfaction ratings improved, and operational efficiency soared. The company's success story demonstrates the power of Appreciative Inquiry in driving positive change and unlocking an organisation's potential.

Preparing for AI in team development

To effectively implement AI in team development, it's essential to set clear objectives, understand team dynamics, and leverage appropriate tools and techniques.

Checklist for preparing for AI in team development:

Define clear objectives

- Identify the specific goals and outcomes for integrating AI into team development
- Align AI objectives with overall organisational strategy and priorities
- Establish measurable metrics and KPIs to track progress and success
- Communicate objectives clearly to all stakeholders involved in the process

Assess team dynamics

- Conduct a thorough analysis of current team dynamics, including strengths and areas for improvement
- Identify the roles, responsibilities, and skill sets of each team member
- Assess team members' readiness and receptivity to AI adoption
- Evaluate the potential impact of AI on team dynamics and collaboration

Select appropriate tools and techniques

- Research and evaluate AI tools and platforms suitable for team development
- Consider factors such as ease of use, scalability, integration with existing systems, and cost-effectiveness
- Identify specific AI techniques, such as machine learning, natural language processing, or predictive analytics, that align with team development objectives
- Develop a comprehensive plan for implementing and integrating AI tools and techniques into team development processes

Secure leadership buy-in

- Present a compelling business case for AI in team development, highlighting the benefits, risks, and potential ROI
- Engage key stakeholders and decision-makers in the planning and implementation process
- Address any concerns or objections raised by leadership, providing clear and convincing responses
- Obtain formal approval and support from leadership to proceed with AI integration in team development

Communicate the process

- Develop a comprehensive communication plan to inform and engage team members throughout the AI adoption process
- Clearly explain the rationale, objectives, and expected outcomes of integrating AI into team development
- Provide regular updates and progress reports to keep team members informed and engaged
- Encourage open communication and feedback from team members, addressing any questions or concerns in a timely and transparent manner

Create a safe and inclusive environment.

- Promote a culture of trust, transparency, and psychological safety within the team
- Encourage open dialogue and active participation from all team members in the AI adoption process
- Provide training and support to help team members understand and adopt AI tools and techniques
- Address any concerns or fears related to AI, such as job security or skill obsolescence, with empathy and clarity
- Celebrate successes and milestones throughout the AI adoption journey, recognising the contributions of all team members

Measuring success

Defining metrics for passion and commitment is crucial for assessing the effectiveness of AI initiatives. This can be done through employee engagement surveys, performance metrics, continuous improvement efforts, regular check-ins, and adjusting strategies based on feedback. Metrics such as Employee Net Promoter Score (NPS), retention rates, productivity measures, innovation metrics, and customer satisfaction scores are helpful when determining the organisation's overall health.

Chapter 7: Using AI to improve the health of your business

AI offers unique opportunities to cultivate passionate and committed teams and drive organisational success.

Enhancing recruitment and talent management

AI-driven recruitment platforms and tools can streamline hiring, allowing businesses to identify and attract top talent more effectively. By analysing vast amounts of data from CV's, job postings, and candidate interactions, AI algorithms can identify qualified candidates who fit well with the company culture.

Personalised learning and development

AI-powered learning platforms can deliver personalised training and development opportunities tailored to each employee's unique needs and preferences. By analysing individual learning styles, preferences, and performance data, these platforms can recommend relevant courses, resources, and activities to help employees develop new skills and advance their careers.

Predictive analytics for employee engagement

AI-driven analytics tools can provide real-time insights into employee sentiment, satisfaction, and engagement levels. By analysing data from surveys, feedback channels, and collaboration platforms, these tools can identify trends, patterns, and potential areas of concern before they escalate, allowing businesses to address issues and enhance employee engagement proactively.

Scenario 6: Lumina Dynamics

Lumina Dynamics, a global technology company, recognised the potential of AI to revolutionise its employee engagement efforts. The company implemented an AI-powered engagement platform that collected and analysed data from various sources, including employee surveys, performance reviews, and social media interactions.

The AI platform, with its ability to provide personalised recommendations, offered real-time insights into employee sentiment, identifying areas of concern and opportunities for improvement. It also guided managers with personalised recommendations on addressing individual employee needs and preferences.

Based on the AI-generated insights, Lumina Dynamics launched targeted initiatives to enhance employee engagement. These included implementing a flexible work policy, launching a mentorship program, and investing in personalised learning and development opportunities.

Lumina Dynamics saw a remarkable rise in employee engagement levels thanks to these AI-driven initiatives. Turnover rates decreased, productivity increased, and the company's reputation as an employer of choice flourished. This success story of Lumina Dynamics is a testament to the transformative power of AI in enhancing employee engagement and developing business success, instilling a sense of optimism about the future of work.

Embracing AI in the workplace

To help current employees accept and work effectively with AI, businesses must proactively support them through education and training, clear communication, empowerment and involvement, skill development and reskilling, ethical considerations and governance, and recognition and reward.

The 25 questions to consider before implementing AI

1. How will AI impact our current workforce, and what strategies can we implement to support employees through this transition?
2. What measures will be taken to ensure job security for employees whose roles may be affected by AI implementation?
3. How will employees be involved in the AI implementation process, and what opportunities will they have to provide input and feedback?
4. What potential impact could AI have on employee morale and job satisfaction, and how can we mitigate any adverse effects?
5. How will we ensure that AI algorithms used in our organisation are free from bias and discrimination?
6. How will AI change how we interact with customers, and how can we maintain a human touch in customer relationships?
7. What data privacy and security measures will be implemented to protect sensitive employee and customer information when implementing AI?
8. How will AI be integrated into our current decision-making processes, and what role will human judgment play?
9. What challenges do we anticipate when integrating AI with our existing systems and processes, and how will we address them?

10. How will AI affect employee autonomy and decision-making capabilities, and how can we ensure employees feel empowered?
11. What are the potential risks associated with AI implementation, and what strategies will we employ to mitigate these risks?
12. How will we provide learning and development opportunities for employees to acquire the skills necessary to work effectively with AI?
13. In what ways can AI help us improve the quality of our products or services, and how will we measure these improvements?
14. How might AI impact employee workload and stress levels, and what measures can we take to promote a healthy work environment?
15. What monitoring and evaluation processes will be established to assess AI's effectiveness and impact on our organisation?
16. How will we ensure that AI implementation aligns with our company's goals, mission, and values?
17. In what ways will AI redefine job roles and responsibilities within our organisation, and how will we support employees through these changes?
18. How can we leverage AI to enhance employee collaboration and teamwork within and across departments?
19. What changes will be needed in our performance evaluation processes to account for AI's impact on employee performance?
20. How can we use AI to improve employee engagement and retention, and what strategies will we implement to achieve this?
21. In what ways can AI support employee well-being and work-life balance, and how will we prioritise these considerations during implementation?
22. How will we ensure that AI promotes diversity and inclusion in our hiring, promotion, and decision-making processes?

23. What steps will we take to build and maintain employee trust and confidence in our organisation's use of AI?

24. What governance structure and regulatory compliance measures will be necessary to ensure AI's responsible and ethical use in our organisation?

25. How will we communicate our AI strategy and progress to employees, stakeholders, and the public, and how will we address any concerns they may raise?

Chapter 8: The importance of a Chief AI Officer and an AI adoption plan

As AI becomes increasingly integral to business operations and strategy, organisations realise the need for dedicated leadership and governance to ensure AI's practical and responsible adoption. This has led to the emergence of the Chief AI Officer (CAIO), a senior executive responsible for overseeing the development and implementation of an organisation's AI strategy. In this chapter, we will delve into the importance of having a CAIO and an AI adoption plan and provide practical advice on ensuring AI's ethical and responsible use in the organisation.

The role of the Chief AI Officer

The Chief AI Officer is a pivotal leadership role that bridges technology and business strategy. The CAIO is entrusted with defining the organisation's AI vision and strategy, aligning AI initiatives with business objectives, and ensuring AI systems' effective implementation and governance. This role brings significant benefits to the organisation, including strategic alignment, effective management, and maximising the value of AI investments, providing a clear path for AI to contribute to the business's success.

Key responsibilities of the CAIO include:

1. Developing and executing the organisation's AI strategy and roadmap

2. Identifying opportunities for AI adoption and value creation

3. Overseeing the development and deployment of AI systems and applications

4. Ensuring the ethical and responsible use of AI, including data privacy and security

5. Building and managing AI talent and partnerships

6. Driving AI literacy and adoption across the organisation

7. Measuring and communicating the business value and impact of AI initiatives

Scenario 7: Smart Invest

Smart Invest, a global financial services company, recognised the strategic importance of AI in driving innovation and competitive advantage. To spearhead its AI transformation, the company appointed a Chief AI Officer (CAIO) to lead the development and execution of its AI strategy.

The CAIO worked closely with business leaders and stakeholders to identify key areas where AI could deliver the most value, such as fraud detection, risk assessment, and personalised customer experiences. The CAIO also established an AI Centre of Excellence (CoE) to promote collaboration, knowledge sharing, and best practices.

Under the CAIO's leadership, Smart Invest implemented a robust AI governance framework to ensure AI's ethical and responsible use. This included establishing clear data privacy and security guidelines, algorithmic transparency and accountability, and regular audits and assessments of AI systems.

As a result of the CAIO's efforts, Smart Invest successfully integrated AI into its core operations and achieved significant business benefits. The company reduced fraud losses by 30%, improved risk assessment accuracy by 25%, and increased customer satisfaction by 20%. The success story of Smart Invest demonstrates the critical role of AI leadership in driving transformative change and business value.

Developing an AI adoption plan

An AI adoption plan is a strategic roadmap that outlines an organisation's approach to implementing AI and ensuring its effective and responsible use. The plan should be aligned with the organisation's overall business strategy and objectives, and AI's unique challenges and opportunities should be considered.

Critical components of an AI adoption plan include:

1. AI vision and objectives
   Defining the organisation's AI vision and objectives and how AI aligns with broader business goals and values.
2. AI use cases and priorities
   Identifying specific AI use cases and priorities based on business needs, feasibility, and potential impact.
3. Data and infrastructure
   Assess the organisation's data and infrastructure readiness for AI and develop a plan to address gaps or limitations.
4. Talent and skills
   Identifying the AI talent and skills required to support AI initiatives and developing a plan to acquire, develop, and retain AI talent.
5. Governance and ethics
   Establishing a governance framework and ethical guidelines for the responsible development, deployment, and use of AI systems.
6. Change management and communication
   Develop a change management and communication plan to ensure AI's smooth adoption and integration across the organisation.

7. Metrics and measurement

   Defining metrics and KPIs to measure the success and impact of AI initiatives and establishing a continuous monitoring and improvement process.

Practical tips for developing an AI adoption plan:

1. Conduct an AI readiness assessment

- Evaluate your organisation's current technology infrastructure, data quality, and data governance practices to identify gaps and areas for improvement.
- Assess your employees' AI literacy and identify training needs to ensure they have the necessary skills to work effectively with AI.
- Analyse your business processes to determine which areas are most suitable for AI implementation and can deliver the most significant value.

2. Engage stakeholders in the planning process

- Identify key stakeholders across various departments, including IT, HR, finance, and business units, who will be impacted by AI adoption.
- Conduct workshops and focus group discussions to gather input and feedback from stakeholders on their needs, concerns, and expectations regarding AI implementation.
- Encourage open communication and collaboration among stakeholders to create a sense of ownership and commitment to the AI adoption plan.

3. Establish clear roles and responsibilities

- Define the roles and responsibilities of each team member involved in the AI adoption process, including project managers, data scientists, IT professionals, and business leaders.
- Assign clear ownership and accountability for each aspect of the AI adoption plan, such as data preparation, model development, testing, and deployment.
- Establish a governance structure that outlines decision-making processes, escalation procedures, and communication channels to ensure smooth coordination and execution of the plan.

4. Develop a phased implementation approach

- Break down the AI adoption plan into manageable phases, starting with pilot projects in areas that have the highest potential for success and impact.
- Set milestones and deliverables for each phase and establish metrics to measure progress and success.
- Gradually scale up AI implementation based on the lessons learned and successes achieved in earlier phases, allowing for necessary adjustments and refinements.

5. Allocate adequate resources and budget:

- Identify the financial, technological, and human resources required for each phase of the AI adoption plan.
- Ensure sufficient budget for AI infrastructure, tools, and talent acquisition or development.
- Consider partnering with external AI partners or consultants to access specialised expertise and resources.

6. Establish data governance and ethics frameworks:

- Develop robust data governance policies and procedures to ensure data quality, security, and privacy throughout AI adoption.
- Establish an ethical framework that outlines principles and guidelines for responsible AI use, including fairness, transparency, and accountability.
- Create a mechanism for employees and stakeholders to report any concerns or issues related to AI ethics and ensure prompt resolution.

7. Provide ongoing training and support

- Develop a comprehensive training program to upskill employees on AI technologies, tools, and processes relevant to their roles.
- Offer ongoing support and resources, such as helpdesk services, knowledge bases, and user communities, to assist employees in troubleshooting and problem-solving.
- Create a culture of continuous learning and encourage employees to share their experiences and best practices with their colleagues.

8. Regularly review and update the plan

- Schedule regular reviews of the AI adoption plan to assess progress, identify challenges, and make necessary adjustments.
- Solicit feedback from stakeholders and employees on their experiences with AI implementation and incorporate their suggestions for improvement.
- Stay informed about the latest AI trends, best practices, and regulatory developments, and update the plan to ensure alignment with industry standards and compliance requirements.

By following these practical tips, organisations can develop a comprehensive and effective AI adoption plan that addresses AI implementation's technical, organisational, and human aspects. Regularly reviewing and updating the plan based on lessons learned and emerging best practices will help ensure its ongoing relevance and success in driving business value and transformation.

Ensuring the ethical use of AI

As AI becomes more pervasive and influential in business and society, ensuring its ethical and responsible use becomes increasingly critical. Organisations have a responsibility to develop and deploy AI systems that are transparent, accountable, fair, and aligned with human values and ethics.

Practical steps organisations can take to ensure the ethical use of AI include:

1. Establishing clear ethical principles and guidelines for AI development and use, aligned with the organisation's values and stakeholder expectations.
2. Conducting regular audits and assessments of AI systems to identify and mitigate potential biases, errors, or unintended consequences.
3. Ensuring transparency and explainability of AI decision-making processes and providing mechanisms for human oversight and intervention when necessary.
4. Implementing solid data privacy and security measures to protect sensitive information and prevent unauthorised access or misuse.
5. Developing a culture of ethical AI, where employees are trained and empowered to identify and raise ethical concerns and considerations in AI projects.

6. Engaging with external stakeholders, such as regulators, industry groups, and civil society organisations, to ensure alignment with emerging standards and best practices for ethical AI.

Scenario 8: Health Compass

Health Compass, a global healthcare technology company, recognised the importance of ethical AI in developing and deploying AI-powered solutions for patient care and medical research. The company established a robust ethical AI framework led by its Chief AI Officer and supported by a cross-functional AI Ethics Committee.

The framework included clear principles and guidelines for data privacy, informed consent, algorithmic fairness, and transparency. The company also implemented regular audits and assessments of its AI systems to identify and mitigate potential biases or unintended consequences.

Health Compass also invested in training and education programs to promote a culture of ethical AI among its employees. These included mandatory ethics training for all AI developers and practitioners and open forums and workshops to discuss ethical considerations and best practices.

As a result of its commitment to ethical AI, Health Compass built trust and confidence among its patients, partners, and stakeholders. The company's AI-powered solutions were recognised for their transparency, fairness, and positive impact on patient outcomes and medical research.

The appointment of a Chief AI Officer and the development of a comprehensive AI adoption plan are critical steps for organisations seeking to harness the transformative potential of AI while ensuring its ethical and responsible use. By proactively addressing the challenges and opportunities presented by AI and putting in place robust governance and moral frameworks, organisations can position themselves for success in the AI-driven future while maintaining the trust and confidence of their stakeholders.

Chapter 9: The future of AI and its impact on business

The rapid advancements in AI will continue to reshape business in profound and unprecedented ways. While AI's transformative potential is already being felt across industries, the true extent of its impact on the future of work and organisational dynamics is yet to be fully realised. In this chapter, we will explore future developments in AI and how they may influence businesses in the coming years, underscoring the importance of proactive planning and adaptability in these changes.

One of the most significant developments is the advent of Artificial General Intelligence (AGI). Unlike the narrow, task-specific AI systems currently dominating the market, AGI refers to creating machines capable of performing any intellectual task a human can. The emergence of AGI would mark a paradigm shift in how businesses operate, enabling the automation of complex decision-making processes and creative problem-solving. This development could lead to the rise of genuinely autonomous organisations, where AI systems work seamlessly with human employees, optimising efficiency and driving innovation at an unprecedented scale.

The implications of AGI for the workforce are both exciting and challenging. On one hand, the automation of higher-level cognitive tasks could free employees from routine work, allowing them to focus on more strategic, value-adding activities. This shift could create new, previously unimagined roles that capitalise on uniquely human skills such as emotional intelligence, creativity, and critical thinking. On the other hand, the widespread adoption of AGI could also result in significant job displacement, particularly in industries heavily reliant on knowledge work. To navigate this transition successfully, businesses must prioritise reskilling and upskilling initiatives, developing a culture of continuous learning and adaptability among their employees.

Personalisation and predictive analytics are another area where AI is poised to make significant strides. As AI algorithms increasingly process vast amounts of data, businesses can deliver hyper-personalised experiences to their customers, anticipating their needs and preferences with uncanny accuracy. This level of personalisation will transform customer engagement and revolutionise decision-making processes across the organisation. By leveraging AI-powered predictive analytics, businesses can optimise supply chain management, forecast market trends, and make data-driven decisions that minimise risk and maximise profitability.

As AI tools and platforms become more accessible and user-friendly, businesses of all sizes can harness their power without requiring extensive technical expertise. This change will level the playing field, enabling smaller organisations to compete with their larger counterparts by leveraging AI to drive efficiency, innovation, and customer satisfaction. However, this increased accessibility also underscores the importance of developing robust governance frameworks and ethical guidelines to ensure the responsible deployment of AI across the business landscape.

The line between human and machine capabilities will become blurred as AI evolves. The rise of brain-computer interfaces and neurotech could usher in a new era of human-machine collaboration, where AI systems can directly augment human cognitive abilities. This symbiotic relationship could lead to unprecedented productivity and innovation as humans and machines work together to tackle complex challenges and drive breakthroughs across industries. However, this integration also raises important questions about the nature of work, the value of human contribution, and the ethical implications of human-machine hybrid approaches to work.

The future of AI also holds the potential for transformative breakthroughs in fields such as healthcare, education, and sustainability. AI-powered diagnostic tools and personalised treatment plans could revolutionise patient care, while intelligent tutoring systems and adaptive learning platforms could reshape the education space. In sustainability, AI could be pivotal in optimising resource management, reducing waste, and developing innovative solutions to global challenges such as climate change and food security. As businesses increasingly align their strategies with these broader societal goals, adopting AI will become a competitive advantage and a moral imperative.

As we look ahead to the future of AI, it is clear that the pace of change will only continue to accelerate. To thrive in this new era, businesses must embrace a proactive and adaptable mindset, continuously reassessing their strategies and workforce capabilities in light of emerging technologies. This requires a deep commitment to ongoing learning and development and a willingness to experiment with new approaches and business models. By embracing a culture of innovation and agility, businesses can position themselves to harness the transformative potential of AI while navigating the challenges and uncertainties that lie ahead.

The future of AI presents a world of boundless possibilities and complex challenges for businesses across industries. As AI systems become more sophisticated and integrated into the fabric of organisational life, the ability to adapt and evolve will become a critical determinant of success. By proactively planning for the impact of AI, investing in employee development, and embracing a culture of continuous learning, businesses can survive and thrive in the age of AI.

Chapter 10: Embracing the future of work

As we conclude this exploration of building passionate and committed teams in the age of AI, it is clear that the journey ahead is both challenging and rewarding. Rapid technological advancements, particularly in AI, present unprecedented opportunities for growth, innovation, and efficiency. However, to fully harness the potential of these tools, we must remain committed to the human element of our organisations.

Throughout this book, we have delved into the strategies and insights necessary to create a culture of engagement, adaptability, and continuous learning. By prioritising the well-being and development of our employees, we lay the foundation for a resilient workforce in the face of change. We are inspired to push the boundaries of what is possible.

As leaders, we guide our organisations through this transformative period with empathy, transparency, and a clear vision for the future. We must be willing to challenge the status quo, embrace new ways of working, and lead by example in our pursuit of excellence. The path ahead may be uncharted, but with the right mindset and tools, we can shape a future where technology and humanity coexist harmoniously, driving unparalleled success.

While this book has provided a comprehensive framework for navigating the age of AI, the learning journey does not end here. The world of work is constantly evolving, and we must remain curious, adaptable, and open to new ideas. To that end, I invite you to join our vibrant community of forward-thinking leaders, where you can connect with like-minded individuals, share your experiences, and continue to grow as a change-maker.

As we embark on this exciting new chapter, let us remember that the power to drive change lies within each of us. By harnessing the potential of AI and automation while never losing sight of the human heart of our organisations, we can create businesses that succeed, inspire, innovate, and make a lasting difference in the world.